Supersonic SOUNDS
PHONEME PRACTICE

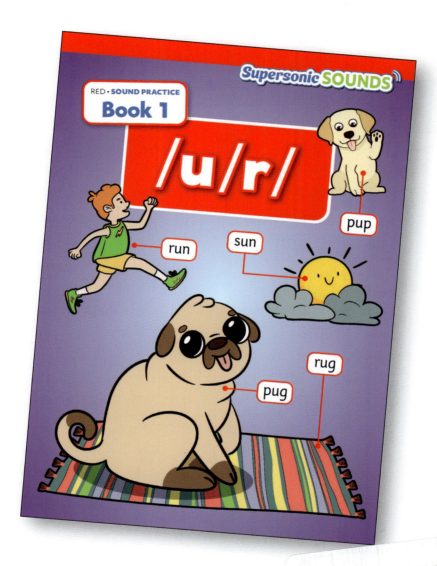

Supersonic SOUNDS

RED · SOUND PRACTICE
Book 1

/u/r/

pup

run

sun

rug

pug

BEARPORT
PUBLISHING

Minneapolis, Minnesota

Teaching Tips

This book focuses on the phonemes **/u/r/**.

Getting Started

- Review the focus phonemes of the book with readers.
- Model the sounds and have readers practice themselves.

Using the Book

- Ask readers to read the words on the pages with the colorful borders, using the focus sounds as their guide.
- Turn the page and check the illustration next to the word to confirm accuracy.
- As you read new words, review the word bank on the left-hand pages of the book.

Reviewing

- Encourage readers to independently reread all of the words on pages 22–23.
- Have them complete the activity on page 24 for continued practice with the focus phonemes.
- Extend the learning by asking readers if they know any other words containing the focus phonemes.

For more information, write to Bearport Publishing, 5357 Penn Avenue South, Minneapolis, MN 55419.

pug

pug

pug

sun

sun

sun

pug

sun

pup

pup

pup

pug

sun

pup

rug

rug

rug

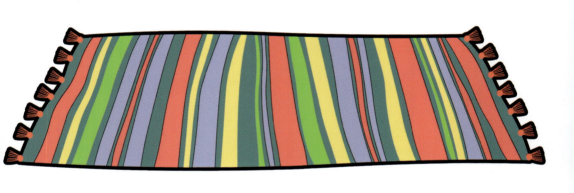

pug

sun

pup

rug

run

run

run

pug

 sun

pup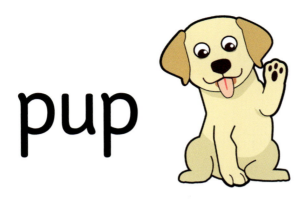

 rug

run

Say the sound. Point to the pictures that start with the /r/ sound.

r